CREATIVE  TOUCHES

Sponging
ETC.

THE HOME DECORATING INSTITUTE®

CREATIVE PUBLISHING international

MINNETONKA, MINNESOTA

Copyright© 1996 Creative Publishing international, Inc. 5900 Green Oak Drive Minnetonka, Minnesota 55343
1-800-328-3895 All rights reserved Printed in U.S.A.

Library of Congress Cataloging-in-Publication Data Sponging etc. p. cm. — (Creative touches)
Includes index. ISBN 0-86573-996-X 1. Texture painting. 2. Interior decoration. I. Creative Publishing international, Inc. II. Series.
TT323.S66 1996 698'.14 — dc20 96-15848

CONTENTS

Getting Started

Primers & Finishes
8

Tools & Supplies
10

Preparing the Surface
12

Water-based Paints
14

Paint Mediums
16

Painting with Glazes

Paint Glaze Basics
21

Strié
23

Combing
25

Rag Rolling
27

Texturizing
31

Texturizing Techniques
33

*More Ideas for Painting
with Glazes*
39

Sponging & Color Washing

Sponge Painting
45

Sponge Painting a Check Design
49

More Ideas for Sponge Painting
52

Color-washed Walls
55

Color-washed Finish for Wood
59

Sponging ETC.

A cozy ambience seems to exist in a room when the walls have a textured appearance. This visual texture is easy and inexpensive to create with a variety of techniques, using water-based paints and glazes. Distinctive patterns can be created with strié or combing techniques, or an overall texture can be developed by rag rolling. Many common household materials can also be used to apply or partially remove paint glaze for unique texturized effects on walls, furniture, and accessories.

Sponge painting, in a choice of styles, can also enhance a painted surface. For a softly pebbled effect, paints are applied and blended, using sea sponges. Using cellulose sponges, a uniform repeating imprint can be made.

As another alternative, color washing can be used to create a soft, translucent effect on painted surfaces or wood. Color-washed walls have a subtle texture and shading, suitable for any decorating style. Used on wood, color washing creates a soft, translucent color that allows the natural tone and grain of the wood to show through.

These techniques and ideas will help you decorate your home with a creative touch. Easy-to-follow instructions with full-color photography help you learn these techniques quickly for results you'll be proud of.

GETTING STARTED

Primers & Finishes

PRIMERS

Some surfaces must be coated with a primer before the paint is applied. Primers ensure good adhesion of paint and are used to seal porous surfaces so paint will spread smoothly without soaking in. It is usually not necessary to prime a nonporous surface in good condition, such as smooth, unchipped, previously painted wood or wallboard. Many types of water-based primers are available; select one that is suitable for the type of surface you are painting.

A. FLAT LATEX PRIMER is used for sealing unfinished wallboard. It makes the surface nonporous so fewer coats of paint are needed. This primer may also be used to seal previously painted wallboard before you apply new paint of a dramatically different color. The primer prevents the original color from showing through.

B. LATEX ENAMEL UNDERCOAT is used for priming most raw woods or woods that have been previously painted or stained. A wood primer closes the pores of the wood, for a smooth surface. It is not used for cedar, redwood, or plywoods that contain water-soluble dyes, because the dyes would bleed through the primer.

C. RUST-INHIBITING LATEX METAL PRIMER helps paint adhere to metal. Once a rust-inhibiting primer is applied, water-based paint may be used on metal without causing the surface to rust.

D. POLYVINYL ACRYLIC PRIMER, or PVA, is used to seal the porous surface of plaster and unglazed pottery, if a smooth paint finish is desired. To preserve the texture of plaster or unglazed pottery, apply the paint directly to the surface without using a primer.

E. STAIN-KILLING PRIMER seals stains like crayon, ink, and grease so they will not bleed through the top coat of paint. It is used to seal knotholes and is the recommended primer for cedar, redwood, and plywood with water-soluble dyes. This versatile primer is also used for glossy surfaces like glazed pottery and ceramic, making it unnecessary to sand or degloss the surface.

FINISHES

Finishes are sometimes used over paint as the final coat. They protect the painted surface with a transparent coating. The degree of protection and durability varies, from a light application of matte aerosol sealer to a glossy layer of clear finish.

F. CLEAR FINISH, such as water-based urethanes and acrylics, may be used over painted finishes for added durability. Available in matte, satin, and gloss, these clear finishes are applied with a brush or sponge applicator. Environmentally safe clear finishes are available in pints, quarts, and gallons (0.5, 0.9, and 3.8 L) at paint supply stores and in 4-oz. and 8-oz. (119 and 237 mL) bottles or jars at craft stores.

G. AEROSOL CLEAR ACRYLIC SEALER, available in matte or gloss, may be used as the final coat over paint as a protective finish. A gloss sealer also adds sheen and depth to the painted finish for a more polished look. Apply aerosol sealer in several light coats rather than one heavy coat, to avoid dripping or puddling. To protect the environment, select an aerosol sealer that does not contain harmful propellants. Use all sealers in a well-ventilated area.

Tools & Supplies

TAPES

When painting, use tape to mask off any surrounding areas. Several brands are available, varying in the amount of tack, how well they release from the surface without damaging the base coat, and how long they can remain in place before removal. You may want to test the tape before applying it to the entire project. The edge of the tape should be sealed tightly to prevent seepage.

PAINT ROLLERS

Paint rollers are used to paint an area quickly with an even coat of paint. Roller pads, available in several nap thicknesses, are used in conjunction with roller frames. Use synthetic or lamb's wool roller pads to apply water-based paints.

A. SHORT-NAP ROLLER PADS with 1/4" to 3/8" (6 mm to 1 cm) nap are used for applying glossy paints to smooth surfaces like wallboard, wood, and smooth plaster.

B. MEDIUM-NAP ROLLER PADS with 1/2" to 3/4" (1.3 to 2 cm) nap are used as all-purpose pads. They give flat surfaces a slight texture.

C. LONG-NAP ROLLER PADS with 1" to 1 1/4" (2.5 to 3.2 cm) nap are used to cover textured areas in fewer passes.

D. ROLLER FRAME is the metal arm and handle that holds the roller pad in place. A wire cage supports the pad in the middle. Select a roller frame with nylon bearings so it will roll smoothly and a threaded end on the handle so you can attach an extension pole.

E. EXTENSION POLE has a threaded end that screws into the handle of a roller frame. Use an extension pole when painting ceilings, high wall areas, and floors.

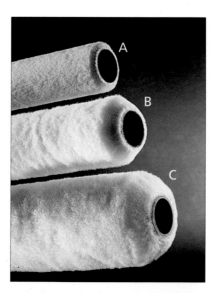

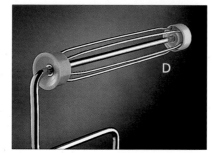

PAINTBRUSHES & APPLICATORS

Several types of paintbrushes and applicators are available, designed for various purposes. Select the correct one to achieve the best quality in the paint finish.

A. SYNTHETIC-BRISTLE paintbrushes are generally used with water-based latex and acrylic paints, while B. NATURAL-BRISTLE brushes are used with alkyd, or oil-based paints. Natural-bristle paintbrushes may be used with water-based paints to create certain decorative effects.

C. BRUSH COMBS remove dried or stubborn paint particles from paintbrushes and align the bristles so they dry properly. To use a brush comb, hold the brush in a stream of water as you pull the comb several times through the bristles from the base to the tips. Use mild soap on the brush, if necessary, and rinse well. The curved side of the tool can be used to remove paint from the roller pad.

Stencil brushes are available in a range of sizes. Use the small brushes for fine detail work in small stencil openings, and the large brushes for larger openings. Either D. SNYTHETIC or E. NATURAL-BRISTLE stencil brushes may be used with acrylic paints.

Artist's brushes are available in several types, including F. FAN, G. LINER, and H. FLAT BRUSHES. After cleaning the brushes, always reshape the head of the brush by stroking the bristles with your fingers. Store artist's brushes upright on their handles or lying flat so there is no pressure on the bristles.

I. SPONGE APPLICATORS are used for a smooth application of paint on flat surfaces.

J. PAINT EDGERS with guide wheels are used to apply paint next to moldings, ceilings, and corners. The guide wheels can be adjusted for proper alignment of the paint pad.

Preparing the Surface

To achieve a high-quality and long-lasting paint finish that adheres well to the surface, it is important to prepare the surface properly so it is clean and smooth. The preparation steps vary, depending on the type of surface you are painting. Often it is necessary to apply a primer to the surface before painting it. For more information about primers, refer to pages 8 and 9.

PREPARING SURFACES FOR PAINTING

SURFACE TO BE PAINTED	PREPARATION STEPS	PRIMER
UNFINISHED WOOD	1. Sand surface to smooth it. 2. Wipe with damp cloth to remove grit. 3. Apply primer.	Latex enamel undercoat.
PREVIOUSLY PAINTED WOOD	1. Clean surface to remove any grease and dirt. 2. Rinse with clear water; allow to dry. 3. Sand surface lightly to degloss and smooth it and to remove any loose paint chips. 4. Wipe with damp cloth to remove grit. 5. Apply primer to any areas of bare wood.	Not necessary, except to touch up areas of bare wood; then use latex enamel undercoat.
PREVIOUSLY VARNISHED WOOD	1. Clean surface to remove any grease and dirt. 2. Rinse with clear water; allow to dry. 3. Sand surface to degloss it. 4. Wipe with damp cloth to remove grit. 5. Apply primer.	Latex enamel undercoat.
UNFINSHED WALLBOARD	1. Dust with hand broom, or vacuum with soft brush attachment. 2. Apply primer.	Flat latex primer.
PREVIOUSLY PAINTED WALLBOARD	1. Clean surface to remove any grease and dirt. 2. Rinse with clear water; allow to dry. 3. Apply primer, only if making a dramatic color change.	Not necessary, except when painting over dark or strong color; then use flat latex primer.
UNPAINTED PLASTER	1. Sand any flat surfaces as necessary. 2. Dust with hand broom, or vacuum with soft brush attachment.	Polyvinyl acrylic primer.
PREVIOUSLY PAINTED PLASTER	1. Clean surface to remove any grease and dirt. 2. Rinse with clear water; allow to dry thoroughly. 3. Fill any cracks with spackling compound. 4. Sand surface to degloss it.	Not necessary, except when painting over dark or strong color; then use polyvinyl acrylic primer.
UNGLAZED POTTERY	1. Dust with brush, or vacuum with soft brush attachment. 2. Apply primer.	Polyvinyl acrylic primer or gesso.
GLAZED POTTERY, CERAMIC & GLASS	1. Clean surface to remove any grease and dirt. 2. Rinse with clear water; allow to dry thoroughly. 3. Apply primer.	Stain-killing primer.
METAL	1. Clean surface with vinegar or lacquer thinner to remove any grease and dirt. 2. Sand surface to degloss it and to remove any rust. 3. Wipe with damp cloth to remove grit. 4. Apply primer.	Rust-inhibiting latex metal primer.
FABRIC	1. Prewash fabric without fabric softener to remove any sizing, if fabric is washable. 2. Press fabric as necessary.	None.

Water-based Paints

A wide variety of paint is available from paint supply stores and craft stores. Each type has advantages that make it especially suitable for certain kinds of painting. All of the following are water-based, making cleanup easy with soap and water. Water-based paints are also safer for the environment than oil-based paints.

LATEX PAINTS

Latex paint is fast drying and durable. In addition to the wide range of premixed colors, latex paint can be custom-mixed by a paint professional. It is available in various finishes, from flat latex for a matte appearance to high-gloss latex with maximum sheen. Low-luster latex enamel paint, sometimes referred to as eggshell enamel, has some sheen and provides good coverage; semigloss has a bit more sheen. The glossier the paint, the more durable it is. Packaged in pints, quarts, and gallons (0.5, 0.9, and 3.8 L), latex paint is suitable for general use in small and large jobs.

Latex paint contains acrylic or vinyl resins or a combination of both. Latex paints of acrylic resins are the highest quality, with vinyl-acrylic blends next in quality, followed by paints consisting solely of vinyl resins. High-quality paints may cost significantly more, but they provide an even, complete coverage and wear longer.

CRAFT ACRYLIC PAINT

Craft acrylic paint contains 100 percent acrylic resins. Generally sold in 2-oz., 4-oz., and 8-oz. (59, 119, and 237 mL) bottles or jars, these premixed acrylics have a creamy brushing consistency and give excellent coverage. They should not be confused with the thicker artist's acrylics used for canvas paintings. Craft acrylic paint can be diluted with water, acrylic extender, or latex paint conditioner (page 16) if a thinner consistency is desired. Craft acrylic paints are available in many colors and in metallic, fluorescent, and iridescent formulas.

CERAMIC PAINTS

Ceramic paints provide a scratch-resistant and translucent finish. They can be heat-hardened in a low-temperature oven to improve their durability, adhesion, and water resistance. Latex and acrylic paints may also be used for painting ceramics, provided the surface is properly primed (page 13).

FABRIC PAINTS

Fabric paints have been formulated specifically for painting on fabric. To prevent excessive stiffness in the painted fabric, avoid a heavy application; the texture of the fabric should show through the paint. Once the paints are heat-set with an iron, the fabric can be machine washed and dry-cleaned. Acrylic paints can also be used for fabric painting; textile medium may be added to the acrylics to make them more pliable on fabric.

Paint Mediums

Paint mediums, such as conditioners, extenders, and thickeners, are often essential for successful results in decorative painting. Available in latex or acrylic, paint mediums are formulated to create certain effects or to change a paint's performance without affecting its color. Some mediums are added directly to the paint, while others are used simultaneously with paint. Mediums are especially useful for latex and acrylic paint glazes (page 21), in that they make an otherwise opaque paint somewhat translucent.

LATEX PAINT CONDITIONER, such as Floetrol®, was developed for use in a paint sprayer with latex paint, but this useful product is also essential in making paint glaze for faux finishes. When paint conditioner is added to paint, it increases the drying or "open" time and extends the wet-edge time to avoid the look of overlapping. The mixture has a lighter consistency and produces a translucent paint finish. Latex paint conditioner may be added directly to either latex or acrylic paint.

TEXTILE MEDIUM is formulated for use with acrylic paint, to make it more suitable for fabric painting. Mixed into the paint, it allows the paint to penetrate the natural fibers of cottons, wools, and blends, creating permanent, washable painted designs. After the fabric is painted, it is heat-set with an iron.

ACRYLIC PAINT EXTENDER thins the paint, increases the open time, and makes paint more translucent.

ACRYLIC PAINT THICKENER increases the drying time of the paint while it thickens the consistency. Thickener can be mixed directly into either acrylic or latex paint. Small bubbles may appear while mixing, but they will disappear as the paint mixture is applied. Thickener is used for painting techniques that require a paint with more body, such as combing.

PAINTING WITH GLAZES

Paint Glaze Basics

Many types of decorative painting require the use of a paint glaze, made by adding paint conditioner (page 16) or paint thickener (page 17) to the paint. With these paint mediums, the drying time of the paint is extended, allowing the additional time needed to manipulate the paint before it sets. The glaze has a creamy texture when wet and forms a translucent top coat once it dries.

Paint glazes have traditionally been made from oil-based paints. These oil glazes are messy to use, difficult to clean up, and noxious. Water-based latex and acrylic glazes, on the other hand, are easier to use, safer for the user and the environment, and lower in cost.

The basic glaze (below) is used for several types of decorative painting, including strié, combing, rag rolling, texturizing, and, sometimes, sponging. The glaze is varied slightly for color washing. Without the use of paint glazes, all of these finishes would be nearly impossible to achieve.

TIPS FOR USING PAINT GLAZE

PROTECT the surrounding area with a drop cloth or plastic sheet and wear old clothing, because working with glaze can be messy.

USE wide painter's tape (page 10) to mask off the surrounding surfaces. Firmly rub the edges of the tape, to ensure that the glaze will not seep under it.

USE a paint roller to apply the glaze when even coverage is desired or when painting a large surface, such as a wall.

USE a paintbrush to apply the glaze when a paint finish with more variation and pattern in the surface is desired or when painting a small item.

USE a sponge applicator to apply the glaze when smooth coverage is desired or when painting a small item.

MANIPULATE the glaze while it is still wet. Although humidity affects the setting time, the glaze can usually be manipulated for a few minutes.

WORK with an assistant when using glaze on a large surface. While one person applies the glaze, the other can manipulate it.

BASIC GLAZE

Mix together the following ingredients:

One part latex or craft acrylic paint in desired sheen.

One part latex paint conditioner, such as Floetrol®.

One part water.

How to apply a strié paint finish

MATERIALS

- Low-luster latex enamel in desired color, for the base coat.
- Latex paint in desired sheen and color, for the glaze.
- Latex paint conditioner, such as Floetrol®.
- Wide natural-bristle brush.
- Soft natural-bristle paintbrush.

1. Prepare the surface (page 13). Apply base coat of low-luster latex enamel; allow to dry. Mix the glaze (page 21); apply over base coat in a vertical section about 18" (46 cm) wide, using paint roller or natural-bristle paintbrush.

2. Drag a dry, wide natural-bristle paintbrush through wet glaze, immediately after glaze is applied; work from top to bottom in full, continuous brush strokes. To keep brush rigid, hold bristles of brush against surface with handle tilted slightly toward you. Repeat until desired effect is achieved.

3. Wipe the paintbrush occasionally on clean, dry rag to remove excess glaze, for a uniform strié look. Or rinse brush in clear water, and wipe dry.

4. Brush the surface lightly after the glaze has dried for about 5 minutes, if softer lines are desired; use a soft natural-bristle brush, and keep brush stokes in the same direction as streaks.

Strié

Strié is a series of irregular streaks in a linear pattern, created by using a paint glaze. Especially suitable for walls, this painting technique can also be used for furniture pieces with flat surfaces.

For large surfaces, it is helpful to work with an assistant. After one person has applied the glaze, the other person brushes through the glaze before it dries, to achieve the strié effect. If you are working alone, limit yourself to smaller sections, if possible, since the glaze must be wet to create this look. If it is necessary to interrupt the process, stop only when a section is completed.

Because it can be messy to apply a strié finish, wear old clothing and protect the surrounding area with drop cloths and wide painter's tape. Firmly rub the edges of the tape, to ensure that the glaze will not seep under it.

Strié lends itself well to tone-on-tone colorations, such as ivory over white or tones of blue, although the color selection is not limited to this look. To become familiar with the technique and test the colors, first apply the finish to a sheet of cardboard, such as mat board.

2

4

How to apply a combed paint finish

MATERIALS

- Low-luster latex enamel paint in desired color, for base coat.

- Latex paint or craft acrylic paint in desired sheen and color, for glaze.

- Latex paint conditioner, for basic glaze; or acrylic paint thickener, for thickened glaze.

- Paintbrush, paint roller, or sponge applicator.

- Combing tool, opposite.

- Clear finish or aerosol clear acrylic sealer, optional.

1. Prepare the surface (page 13). Apply a base coat of low-luster latex enamel to surface, using a sponge applicator, paintbrush, or paint roller. Allow to dry.

2. Mix basic glaze (page 21) or thickened glaze (opposite); apply to small area at a time, using a sponge applicator, paintbrush, or paint roller. Drag combing tool through wet glaze to create pattern. Allow to dry. Apply clear finish or sealer, if desired.

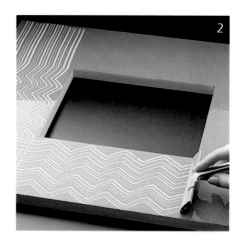

Combing

Combing is a decorative painting technique that has been used for many years, as is evident by the number of antiques with this finish. For this technique, a paint glaze is applied over a base coat of paint. Narrow lines or stripes in the finish are created as you drag the teeth of a comb through the paint glaze, removing some of the glaze to reveal the base coat of paint. For a pronounced effect, the color of the paint glaze may contrast with that of the base coat.

A variety of combed patterns, such as wavy lines, scallops, crisscrosses, zigzags, and basket weaves, can be created. If you are unsatisfied with a particular pattern, the glaze can be wiped off while it is still wet, then reapplied; or the wet glaze can be smoothed out with a paintbrush, then combed into a different pattern.

You may use either the basic paint glaze (page 21) or a thickened glaze of two parts paint and one part acrylic paint thickener. The basic glaze produces a more translucent look and works well on walls and other surfaces without adding texture to the surface. The thickened glaze gives an opaque look with more distinct lines and texture.

A. RUBBER OR METAL COMBING TOOLS, available at craft and art stores, work well for this paint finish. If desired, you can make your own comb by cutting V grooves into a B. RUBBER SQUEEGEE or C. PIECE OF MAT BOARD.

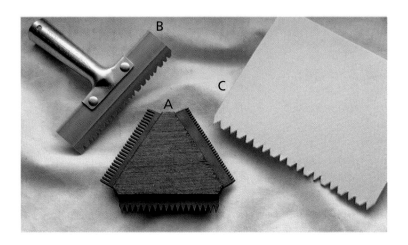

Rag Rolling

Rag rolling is a painting technique that gives a rich, textural look with an allover mottled effect. It works well for walls and other flat surfaces, such as dresser tops and drawers, shelves, bookends, and doors. The basic paint glaze on page 21 can be used in either of the two techniques for rag rolling, *ragging-on* and *ragging-off.*

In ragging-on, a rag is saturated in the prepared paint glaze, wrung out, rolled up, and then rolled across a surface that has been base-coated with low-luster latex enamel paint. Rag-on a single application of glaze over the base coat, for a bold pattern. Or, for a more subtle, blended look, rag-on two or more applications of glaze.

In ragging-off, apply a coat of paint glaze over the base coat, using a paintbrush or paint roller; then roll up a rag and roll it over the wet glaze to remove some of the glaze. This process may be repeated for more blending, but you must work fast, because the glaze dries quickly.

If you are using the ragging-off method on large surfaces, such as walls, it is helpful to have an assistant. After one person applies the glaze, the second person can rag-off the area before the glaze dries. While it is not necessary to complete the entire room in one session, it is important that you complete an entire wall.

With either method, test the technique and the colors that you intend to use on a large piece of cardboard, such as mat board, before you start the project. Generally, a lighter color is used for the base coat, with a darker color for the glaze.

Feel free to experiment with the technique as you test it, perhaps rag rolling two different glaze colors over the base coat. Or try taping off an area, such as a border strip, and rag rolling a second or third color within the taped area.

Because the glaze can be messy to work with, apply a wide painter's tape around the area to be painted and use drop cloths to protect the surrounding surfaces. Wear old clothes and rubber gloves, and keep an old towel nearby to wipe your hands after you wring out the rags.

How to apply a rag-rolled paint finish using the ragging-on method

MATERIALS

- Low-luster latex enamel paint, for base coat.

- Latex or craft acrylic paint and latex paint conditioner, for glaze; 1 qt. (0.9 L) of each is sufficient for the walls of a 12 ft. x 14 ft. (3.7 x 4.33 m) room.

- Paint pail; rubber gloves; old towel; lint-free rags, about 24" (61 cm) square.

1. Prepare surface (page 13). Apply a base coat of low-luster latex enamel, using paintbrush or paint roller. Allow to dry.

2. Mix basic glaze (page 21) in pail. Dip lint-free rag into glaze, saturating entire rag; wring out well. Wipe excess glaze from hands with old towel.

3. Roll up the rag irregularly; then fold in half to a width equal to both hands.

4. Roll the rag over surface, working upward at varying angles. Rewet rag whenever necessary, and wring out.

5. Repeat the application, if more coverage is desired.

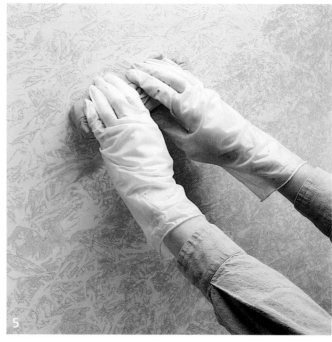

How to apply a rag-rolled paint finish using the ragging-off method

1. Apply base coat of low-luster latex enamel, using paintbrush or paint roller. Allow to dry.

2. Mix basic glaze (page 21); pour into a paint tray. Apply the glaze over the base coat, using paint roller or paint pad.

3. Roll up lint-free rag irregularly; fold in half to width of both hands. Roll the rag through the wet glaze, working upward at varying angles.

COLOR EFFECTS

As shown in the examples below, the color of the base coat is not affected when the ragging-on method is used. With the ragging-off method, the color of the base coat is changed, because the glaze is applied over the entire surface, and then some glaze is removed with a rag to soften the background.

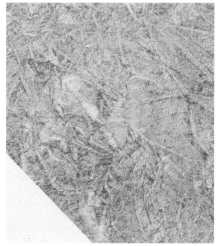

RAGGING-ON is used, applying aqua glaze over a white base coat. The white base coat remains unchanged.

RAGGING-OFF is used, applying aqua glaze over a white base coat. The white base coat is covered with the glaze, then appears as a lighter aqua background when some of the glaze is removed.

RAGGING-ON AND RAGGING-OFF are both used. First a taupe glaze is ragged-on over a white base coat. Then a rust glaze is ragged-off, changing the white base coat to a lighter shade of rust.

Texturizing

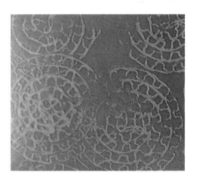

In addition to the methods for strié, combing, and rag rolling, numerous household items and painting supplies can be used with paint glaze to achieve finishes that have visual texture. Rolled or bent pieces of corrugated cardboard cheesecloth, crumpled paper, raffia, plastic wrap, carved potatoes, and scrub brushes create interesting textured effects. The list of items is as endless as your imagination.

For these finishes, use the basic glaze and instructions on page 21. You may apply a coat of glaze directly to the surface, then manipulate it or partially remove it by dabbing the glaze with the item or items you have selected. Or using the alternate method, the glaze may be applied to the selected items, then printed onto the surface. To become familiar with the methods and determine which effects you prefer, experiment with both methods, using a variety of items.

Apply a base coat of paint, using a good-quality low-luster latex enamel, before you apply the glaze. The base coat and the glaze may be in contrasting colors, such as emerald green over white. For a more subtle look, try a tone-on-tone effect, such as two shades of blue, or choose colors that are similar in intensity, such as deep red over deep purple. For even more possibilities, the process can be repeated, using one or more additional colors of glaze. This adds even more visual interest and is especially suitable for small accessories.

LEFT: ACCESSORIES have a variety of textural effects, created using folded cheesecloth for the vase, rolled corrugated cardboard for the bowl, and single-face corrugated cardboard for the tray.

MATERIALS

- Low-luster latex enamel paint in desired color, for base coat.
- Latex or acrylic paint in desired sheen and color, for glaze.
- Latex paint conditioner, such as Floetrol®.
- Items selected for creating the textural effect.

How to apply a texturized paint finish

1. Prepare surface (page 13). Apply a base coat of low-luster latex enamel, using sponge applicator, paintbrush, or paint roller. Allow to dry.

2. Mix glaze (page 21). Apply glaze to a small area at a time, using sponge applicator, paintbrush, or paint roller. A heavier coat of glaze gives a more opaque finish, and a light coat, a more translucent finish.

3. Texturize glaze by dabbing, rolling, or dragging items in the glaze to create patterns; rotate item, if desired, to vary the look. Replace the item as necessary, or wipe the excess glaze from item occasionally.

ALTERNATE METHOD. Follow step 1, above. Then apply glaze to selected item, using a sponge applicator, paintbrush, or paint roller; blot on paper towel or cardboard. Dab, roll, or drag glaze-covered item over base coat, to apply glaze to surface randomly or in desired pattern.

Texturizing techniques

CARDBOARD. Rolled corrugated cardboard is secured by taping it together. Use corrugated end to make design in coat of wet glaze (A). Or apply glaze directly to cardboard; blot, and print designs on surface (B).

Single-face corrugated cardboard is cut to the desired shape. To make design, press corrugated side in coat of wet glaze (C). Or apply glaze directly to corrugated side; blot, and print designs on surface (D).

Continued

Texturizing techniques

CHEESECLOTH. Fold cheesecloth into a flat pad and press into coat of wet glaze (A). Or apply glaze directly to a folded flat pad of cheesecloth, then imprint the cheesecloth onto the surface (B).

PAPER. Crumple paper and press into coat of wet glaze (C). Or apply glaze directly to paper; press onto the surface, crumpling the paper (D).

PLASTIC WRAP. Wrinkle plastic wrap slightly and place over coat of wet glaze; press lightly, and peel off (A). Or apply glaze directly to plastic wrap. Then place plastic wrap on the surface, folding and crinkling it; peel off (B).

FAN BRUSH. Press brush into wet glaze, making uniform rows of fan-shaped impressions (C). Or apply glaze directly to fan brush, and print fan-shaped designs on surface (D).

Continued

Texturizing techniques

(CONTINUED)

COARSE FABRIC. Fanfold a narrow length of burlap or other coarse fabric into a thick pad; apply glaze. Flip folds to back of pad as they become saturated, exposing fresh fabric for texturizing (A). Or, crumple a piece of coarse fabric into loose, irregular folds; apply glaze. Recrumple or start with a fresh piece as fabric becomes saturated (B).

TWINE OR STRING. To texturize with a distinctive pattern, use the twine or string as it comes in a ball. Apply glaze; press onto surface, turning ball or unwinding twine or string as areas become saturated (C). Or, wind string or twine erratically into a tangle for more irregularly shaped pattern (D). Apply glaze and press onto surface.

COARSE NETTING (A). Apply glaze to netting balls, such as those found in bath shops; press onto surface. Netting will not absorb the glaze, so will not become saturated.

SPATTERING (B). Protect the work surface with drop cloths. Mix paints in small cups, combining two parts paint with one part water. Dip tip of brush into paint; remove excess paint on edge of cup. Hold stick and brush over project; strike brush handle against stick to spatter paint. Work from top to bottom in wide strips. Allow first color of paint to dry. Repeat steps for each color, as desired.

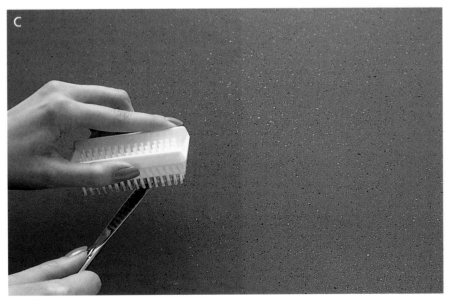

SPECKING (C). Dip ends of stiff-bristled brush into thinned paint. Tap brush onto piece of paper to remove excess paint. Hold brush over surface to be painted; flick bristles toward you using knife or finger, spraying paint away from you. The closer to the surface the brush is held, the finer the spattering and the more control you have.

More ideas for painting with glazes

LEFT: GLAZE FINISHES (page 21) are combined to decorate this small jewelry box. The top and sides of the box are sponge painted; from top to bottom, the drawers are painted using the ragging-on, texturizing, and combing techniques.

CENTER: SPECIALTY PAINT ROLLER quickly creates visual texture on a fabric surface. The roller can be used on hard surfaces, as well.

RIGHT: COMBED SURFACE emphasizes the unique shape of this vase.

Continued

TOP: RAG ROLLING adds textural interest to walls, furniture, and accessories. This tabletop was painted by ragging-off.

LEFT: MAGAZINE RACK is painted by applying two colors of paint, using the ragging-on method (page 28). A final coat of aerosol clear acrylic sealer adds luster and provides a durable finish.

OPPOSITE: VISUAL TEXTURE was applied to this wall, using crumpled burlap.

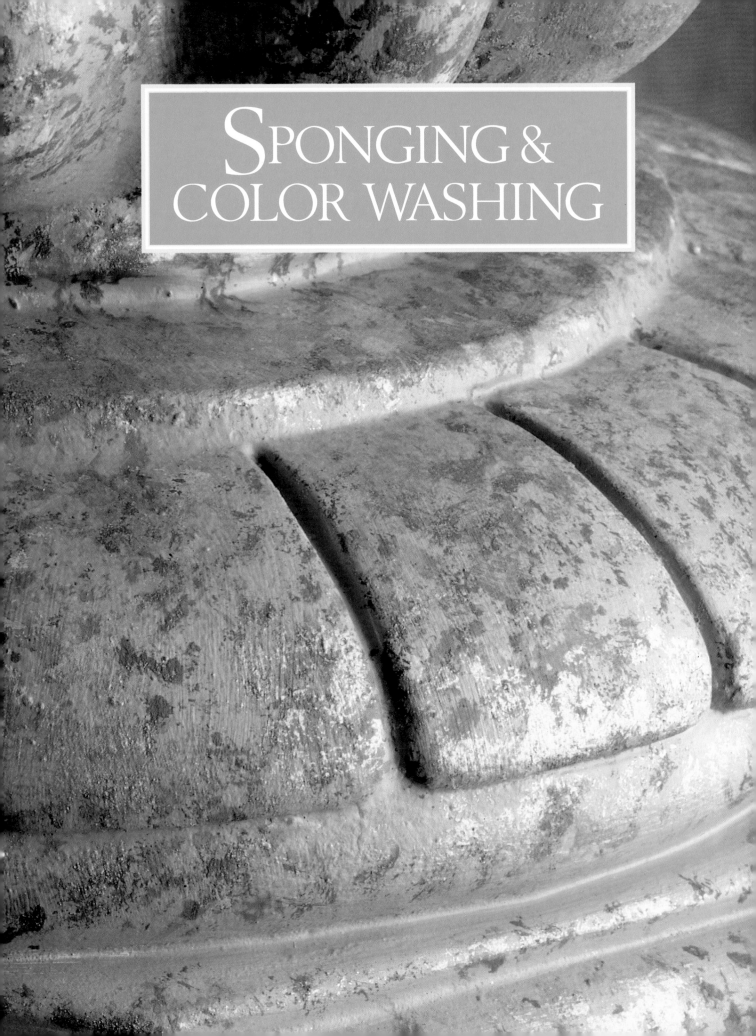

SPONGING &
COLOR WASHING

*S*ponge *Painting*

Sponge painting produces a soft, mottled effect and is one of the easiest techniques to use. To achieve this paint finish, use a natural sea sponge to dab paint onto a surface. Cellulose or synthetic sponges should not be used because they tend to leave identical impressions with hard, defined edges.

The sponged look can be varied, depending on the number of paint colors applied, the sequence in which you apply the colors, and the distance between the sponge impressions. You can use semigloss, low-luster, or flat latex paint for the base coat and the sponging. Or for a translucent finish, use a paint glaze that consists of paint, paint conditioner, and water; make the glaze as on page 21.

To create stripes, borders, or panels, use painter's masking tape to mask off the desired areas of the surface after the first color of sponged paint is applied. Then apply another color to the unmasked areas.

Fabric may be sponge painted, using fabric paint (page 15) or craft acrylic paint mixed with textile medium (page 17). Prewash fabric to remove any sizing, if fabric is washable, and press well to remove wrinkles. Apply paint with sea sponge, as in step 2 on page 46, but do not blot with a wet sponge. When the fabric is dry, heat-set the paint using a dry iron and a press cloth.

How to sponge paint

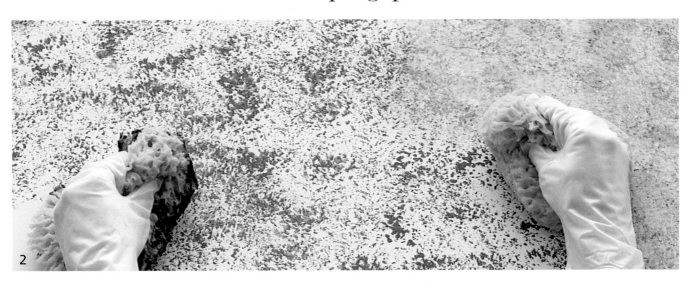

MATERIALS

- Craft acrylic or latex paints in desired sheens and colors, for base coat and for sponging.
- Natural sea sponge.
- Painter's masking tape.
- Carpenter's level, for painting stripes, borders, or panels.

1. Prepare surface (page 13). Apply base coat of desired color. Allow to dry. Rinse sea sponge in water to soften it; squeeze out most of the water. Saturate sponge with paint or with paint glaze (page 21). Blot the sponge lightly on paper towel.

2. Press sponge repeatedly onto surface, as shown at left; work quickly in small areas, and change position of sponge often. Blot paint on surface immediately, using wet sea sponge in other hand, as shown at right; this causes the paint to bleed, for a softened, blended look. Some of the paint is removed with the wet sponge.

3. Continue to apply the first paint color to entire project, blotting with moist sponge. Repeat steps with one or more additional colors of paint, if desired. Allow paint to dry between colors.

4. Optional feathering. Apply final color of paint, using a light, sweeping motion instead of dabbing.

How to sponge paint stripes, borders, or panels

1. Follow steps 1 to 3, opposite. Allow paint to dry thoroughly. Mark light plumb line, using a pencil and carpenter's level. Position first row of painter's masking tape along this line.

2. Measure and position remaining rows of painter's masking tape to mark stripes, borders, or panel areas.

3. Apply second paint color to the unmasked areas of the surface. Allow paint to dry.

4. Remove the painter's masking tape, revealing two variations of sponge painting.

COLOR EFFECTS

When related colors are used for sponge painting, such as two warm colors or two cool colors, a harmonious look is achieved. For a bolder and more unexpected look, sponge paint in a combination of warm and cool colors.

WARM COLORS like yellow and orange blend together for an exciting effect.

COOL COLORS like green and blue blend together for a tranquil effect.

WARM AND COOL COLORS like yellow and blue combine boldly, but sponge painting softens the effect.

Sponge Painting a Check Design

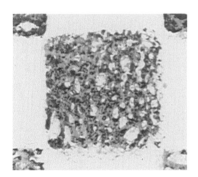

For a dramatic check pattern on walls, apply paint with squares of cellulose sponge. For easier application of the paint, glue the sponge to a piece of plywood and use it as a stamp. As a final step, add more dimension and color to the design, if desired, by lightly stamping another paint color over the checks. For this second paint color, use a square stamp of the same size, or make a stamp in a smaller size or shape.

For even rows, the check pattern works best for walls that have squared corners and ceiling lines. A plumb line may be used as a vertical guide. Plan to start painting at the most prominent corner of the room and work in both directions so full squares will meet at that corner. You may want to divide the dominant wall evenly into checks across the width of the wall.

Flat latex or low-luster latex enamel paint may be used for painting walls. To provide a more durable finish on cabinets and furniture, use a gloss enamel.

How to sponge paint a check design

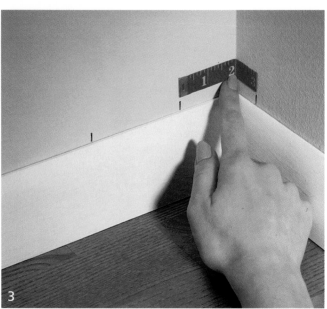

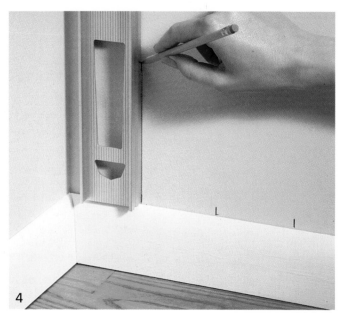

MATERIALS

- Latex paint in desired background color, for base coat.
- Latex paint in one or more colors, for stamped design.
- Large cellulose sponges.
- Scraps of ¼" (6 mm) plywood; hot glue gun and glue sticks.
- Thin transparent Mylar® sheets.

1. Cut cellulose sponge into the desired size of square for check design; cut plywood to same size. Make a stamp by securing sponge to plywood, using hot glue. Make one stamp for each color and shape in design.

2. Prepare surface (page 13). Apply base coat of paint in desired background color; allow to dry. Mark placement for first row of design, at bottom of wall, using pencil. For example, for a 3" (7.5 cm) stamp, lightly mark wall at 3" (7.5 cm) intervals. (Pencil markings are exaggerated to show detail.)

3. Mark the wall to corner. If full width of the design does not fit into the corner, measure around corner, and mark. Then continue marking full widths. Mark spaces on all walls.

4. Lightly mark a plumb line on wall, at the first marking from corner, using a level and pencil. Or hang a string at corner, using a pushpin near top of wall; weight string at bottom so it acts as a plumb line.

5. Apply paint to the sponge, using paintbrush. Stamp the bottom row of checks onto the wall.

6. Continue to stamp rows of checks, working up from bottom of wall and using previous row and plumb line as horizontal and vertical guides. If full stamped design does not fit into corners or at top of wall, leave area unpainted at this time.

7. Allow paint to dry. To fill in areas with partial stamped designs, place a piece of Mylar over previously painted checks to protect wall. Stamp design up to corners and top of wall, overlapping stamp onto Mylar. Allow paint to dry.

8. Add dimension and color to check design, if desired, using stamp of same size and shape as checks, or cut to a different size and shape. Apply another paint color, stamping very lightly over painted checks. Dispose of used stamps.

More ideas for sponge painting

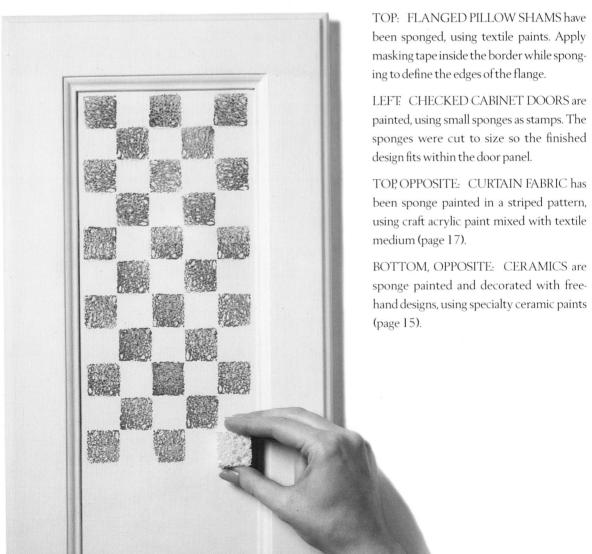

TOP: FLANGED PILLOW SHAMS have been sponged, using textile paints. Apply masking tape inside the border while sponging to define the edges of the flange.

LEFT: CHECKED CABINET DOORS are painted, using small sponges as stamps. The sponges were cut to size so the finished design fits within the door panel.

TOP, OPPOSITE: CURTAIN FABRIC has been sponge painted in a striped pattern, using craft acrylic paint mixed with textile medium (page 17).

BOTTOM, OPPOSITE: CERAMICS are sponge painted and decorated with free-hand designs, using specialty ceramic paints (page 15).

Color-washed Walls

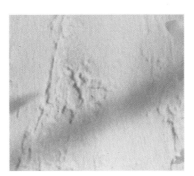

Color washing is an easy paint finish that gives walls a translucent, watercolored look. It adds visual texture to flat drywall surfaces, and it further emphasizes the already textured surface of a plaster or stucco wall.

In this technique, a color-washing glaze is applied in a cross-hatching fashion over a base coat of low-luster latex enamel, using a natural-bristle paintbrush. As the glaze begins to dry, it can be softened further by brushing the surface with a dry natural-bristle paintbrush. Complete one wall before moving on to the next or before stopping. Store any remaining glaze in a reclosable container between painting sessions.

The color-washing glaze can be either lighter or darker than the base coat. For best results, use two colors that are closely related or consider using a neutral color like beige or white for either the base coat or the glaze. Because the glaze is messy to work with, cover the floor and furniture with drop cloths and apply painter's tape along the ceiling and moldings.

COLOR-WASHING GLAZE

Mix together the following ingredients:

One part flat latex paint.

One part latex paint conditioner.

Two parts water.

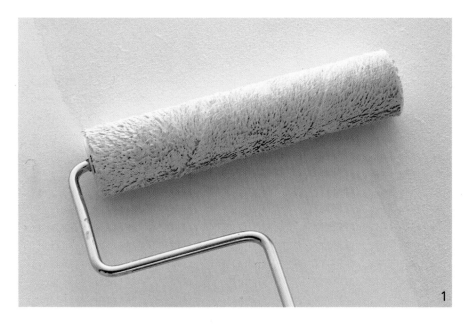

How to color wash walls

MATERIALS

- Low-luster latex enamel paint, for base coat.
- Flat latex paint, for color-washing glaze.
- Latex paint conditioner, for color-washing glaze.
- Paint roller.
- Two 3" to 4" (7.5 to 10 cm) natural-bristle paintbrushes for each person.
- Drop cloths; painter's tape.

1. Prepare the surface (page 13). Apply a base coat of low-luster latex enamel paint in the desired color, using a paint roller. Allow to dry.

2. Mix the color-washing glaze (page 55). Dip paintbrush into the glaze; remove excess glaze against rim of the container. Apply the glaze to wall in cross-hatching manner, beginning in one corner. The more you brush over the surface, the softer the appearance.

3. Brush over the surface, if desired, using a dry natural-bristle paintbrush, to soften the look. Wipe excess glaze from the brush as necessary.

COLOR EFFECTS

Select colors for the base coat and the glaze that are closely related, or use at least one neutral color. A darker glaze over a lighter base coat gives a mottled effect. A lighter glaze over a darker base coat gives a chalky or watercolored effect.

Apply a darker top coat, such as a medium turquoise, over a lighter base coat, such as white (A).

Apply a lighter top coat, such as white, over a darker base coat, such as coral (B).

Apply two shades of a color, such as a medium blue top coat over a light blue base coat (C).

Color-washed Finish for Wood

A subtle wash of color gives an appealing finish to wooden cabinets and accessories. This finish works for all decorating styles, from contemporary to country.

For color washing, a flat latex or acrylic paint is diluted with water. Applied over unfinished or stained wood, the color wash allows the natural wood tone and grain to show through. The lighter the original surface, the lighter the finished effect. To lighten a dark surface, first apply a white color wash, followed by a color wash in the desired finish color.

If you are applying a color wash to a varnished surface, remove any grease or dirt by washing the surface. It is important to roughen the varnish by sanding it, so the wood will accept the color-wash paint.

BELOW: COLOR-WASHED STRIPES have been applied to a wooden charger for a cheerful country accent.

How to apply a color-washed finish

MATERIALS

- Flat latex paint.
- Matte or low-gloss clear acrylic sealer or finish.
- Paintbrush.
- 220-grit sandpaper.
- Tack cloth.

1. Prepare wood surface by cleaning and sanding it; if surface is varnished, roughen it with sandpaper. Wipe with damp cloth.

2. Mix one part flat latex paint to four parts water. Apply to wood surface, brushing in direction of wood grain and working in an area no larger than 1 sq. yd. (0.95 sq. m) at a time. Allow to dry for 5 to 10 minutes.

3. Wipe surface with clean, lint-free cloth to partially remove paint, until desired effect is achieved. If the color is too light, repeat the process. Allow to dry. Lightly sand surface with 220-grit sandpaper to soften the look; wipe with damp cloth.

4. Apply one to two coats of clear acrylic sealer or finish, sanding lightly between coats.

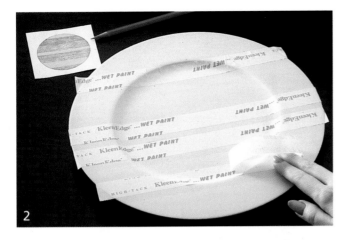

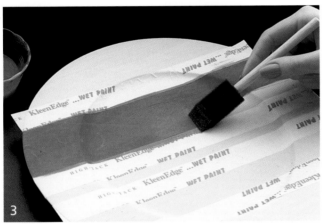

How to apply color-washed stripes

MATERIALS

- Craft acrylic paints in desired colors.
- 100-grit, 150-grit, and 220-grit sandpaper.
- Damp cloth.
- Paintér's masking tape.
- Sponge applicator.
- Clear finish or aerosol clear acrylic sealer.

1. Sand the charger in the direction of the wood grain, using 150-grit sandpaper, then 220-grit sandpaper. Remove any grit, using a damp cloth.

2. Determine the desired color and width of each stripe in the charger, repeating colors as desired. Using painter's masking tape, mask off each side of stripes for the first paint color.

3. Dilute the paints, one part paint to two parts water. Apply the first paint color lightly to the masked stripes, using a sponge applicator; use paint sparingly. Allow to dry; remove tape.

4. Repeat steps 2 and 3 for each remaining paint color, allowing the paint to dry between colors.

5. Sand painted charger in the direction of wood grain, using 100-grit sandpaper, to give a worn appearance to the surface, especially sanding along outer and inner edges of the rim.

6. Apply a coat of clear finish or aerosol clear acrylic sealer to the charger. Apply additional coats as desired, sanding smooth between coats.

Index

A

Acrylic paint extender, 17

Acrylic paint thickener, 17

Aerosol clear acrylic sealer, 9

Applicators and paintbrushes, 11

Artist's brushes, 11

B

Borders, sponge painting, 47

Brush combs, 11

Brushes, for painting, 11

C

Check design, sponge painting, 47

Clear finish, 9

Color washing,

    finish for wood, 59-61

    walls, 55-57

Combing, 24-25, 39

Conditioner, latex paint, 16

Craft acrylic paint, 15

D

Design, check, sponge painting, 49-51

E

Edgers, paint, 11

Extender, acrylic paint, 17

Extension pole, paint rollers, 10

F

Fabric paints, 15

Finish for wood, color washing, 59-61

Finishes, 9

Flat latex primer, 8, 13

G

Glazes, painting with,

    basics, 21

    combing, 24-25, 39

    ideas for, 39-41

    rag rolling, 27-29, 41

    strié, 22-23

    texturizing, 31-37

I

Ideas,

    painting with glazes, 39-41

    sponge painting, 52-53

L

Latex enamel undercoat, 8, 13

Latex paint conditioner, 16

Latex paints, 14

M

Mediums, paint, 16-17

Metal primer, rust-inhibiting latex, 8, 13

P

Paint edgers, 11

Paint mediums, 16-17

Paint rollers, 10

Paintbrushes and applicators, 11

Paints and glazes, water-based, 14-15

Panels, sponge painting, 47

Pole, extension, paint rollers, 10

Polyvinyl acrylic primer (PVA), 8, 13

Preparing the surface, 12-13

Primers, 8-9, 13

R

Rag rolling, 27-29, 41

Ragging-off, 27, 29, 41

Ragging-on, 27-29

Rollers, paint, 10

Rust-inhibiting latex metal primer, 8, 13

S

Sealer, aerosol clear acrylic, 9

Spattering, 37

Specking, 37

Sponge applicators, 11

Sponge painting, 45-47

    check design, 49-51

    ideas for, 52-53

Stain-killing primer, 9, 13

Stencil brushes, 11

Strié, 22-23

Stripes,

    color washing, 59, 61

    sponge painting, 47

Supplies and tools, 10-11

Surface, preparing, 12-13

T

Tapes, 10

Textile medium, 17

Texturizing, 31-37

Thickener, acrylic paint, 17

Tools and supplies, 10-11

U

Undercoat, latex enamel, 8, 13

W

Walls, color washing, 55-57

Wood, color-washed finish for, 59-61

Creative Touches™

Group Executive Editor: Zoe A. Graul

Managing Editor: Elaine Johnson

Editor: Linda Neubauer

Associate Creative Director: Lisa Rosenthal

Senior Art Director: Delores Swanson

Contributing Art Director: Judith Meyers

Computer Design: Mark Jacobson

Copy Editor: Janice Cauley

Desktop Publishing Specialist: Laurie Kristensen

Sample Production Manager: Carol Olson

Studio Manager: Marcia Chambers

Print Production Manager: Patt Sizer

SPONGING ETC.
Created by: The Editors of Creative Publishing international, Inc.

Also available in the Creative Touches™ series:

Stenciling Etc., Stone Finishes Etc., Valances Etc.,
Painted Designs Etc., Metallic Finishes Etc., Swags Etc.,
Papering Projects Etc.

The Creative Touches™ series draws from the individual titles of
The Home Decorating Institute®. Individual titles are also available from the publisher and in bookstores and fabric stores.

Printed on American paper by:
 R. R. Donnelley & Sons Co.
1 0 9 8 7 6

Creative Publishing international, Inc. offers a variety of how-to
books.

For information write:

 Creative Publishing international, Inc.

 Subscriber Books

 5900 Green Oak Drive

 Minnetonka, MN 55343